MW01109669

Searching for the Truth

How Christianity Compares to World Religions

Judaism Islam New Age Buddhism Cults Hinduism

Group
Loveland, Colorado

Group resources actually work!

This Group resource incorporates our R.E.A.L. approach to ministry. It reinforces a growing friendship with Jesus, encourages long-term learning, and results in life transformation, because it's

Relational
Learner-to-learner interaction enhances learning and builds Christian friendships.

Experiential
What learners experience through discussion and action sticks with them up to 9 times longer than what they simply hear or read.

Applicable
The aim of Christian education is to equip learners to be both hearers and doers of God's Word.

Learner-based
Learners understand and retain more when the learning process takes into consideration how they learn best.

Searching for the Truth: How Christianity Compares to World Religions

Copyright © 2002 Group Publishing, Inc.

Visit our Web site: **www.group.com**

Credits

Contributing Authors: Mike DeVries, Karl Leuthauser, Dave Ricketts, Siv M. Ricketts, Christina Schofield, Vicki L.O. Witte, and Paul Woods
Editor: Kelli B. Trujillo
Creative Development Editor: Amy Simpson
Chief Creative Officer: Joani Schultz
Copy Editor: Janis Sampson
Art Director/Designer: Becky Hawley Design
Assistant Art Director: Jean Bruns
Cover Art Director: Jeff A. Storm
Cover Designer: Blukazoo Studio
Cover Photographer: Daniel Treat
Illustrator: Becky Hawley Design
Production Manager: Dodie Tipton

ISBN 978-0-7644-2394-9

Printed in the United States of America.

10 9 8 7 6 5   11 10 09 08

Table of Contents

Introduction

How did I get here?

What is my purpose in the world?

What is the meaning of life?

Do you ever feel like you're searching for the truth? Trying to find the right answer in a world of religious options? So many people, groups, and religions claim to have the truth...but they can't *all* be true, can they?

Looking for answers to spiritual questions can be confusing, and it can be even tougher to get straight answers about the similarities and differences between various religious beliefs. *Searching for the Truth* will give you a chance to see in black and white how other world religions compare to the basic beliefs of Christianity.

You can read this booklet straight through from cover to cover or just flip to the specific religion that you're interested in learning more about. Use the "Sum It Up!" pages at the end of each section to get an overview of the beliefs of each religion. Compare the "Sum It Up!" sections to see how the religions differ from each other. Take notes on your observations or questions.

A very famous and powerful man once asked a question that has been echoed by people throughout the centuries—a question that you too may be asking. Pontius Pilate asked Jesus, "What is truth?" (John 18:38).

It's a good question to have, but it's not enough to just ask the question. It's only through *searching* for the truth that you'll come to know what you truly believe.

Karma, Dharma, AND Reincarnation

A Closer Look at Hinduism

Today there are over 400 million Hindus in the world, mostly living in India, with many in Asia, Africa, and the West Indies. Hinduism has gained momentum in Western cultures and is the foundation of Buddhism and the New Age movement. Hinduism centers around a belief in a universal spirit, reincarnation, and a life of duty and devotion.

A Universal Spirit

Hindus put their faith in Brahman, the supreme god. Hindu followers also worship many lesser gods similar in power and function to angels. Hindus view god as the "Absolute," an impersonal, universal spirit. Every person makes up part of that spirit—parts of god, like drops of water in the ocean. Coming to grips with that realization is the first step toward a Hindu's "salvation" that is reached through philosophy and knowledge. The Hindu idea that all is one and all is god equates humans with animals and even inanimate objects.

Hindus have little need for Jesus. Though they accept him as a teacher, or guru, they claim he has nothing to do with salvation and deny that he rose from the dead. Hindus don't acknowledge the existence of the Holy Spirit.

Reincarnation

The goal of Hinduism is for souls to be cleansed from earthly sins so they can return to Brahman, the Hindu god. This is tricky because the soul may add new sins instead of subtracting them in a lifetime. A person's karma comes from good or bad deeds done in a lifetime. If one's good deeds outweigh the bad, the person has good karma. If the bad deeds outnumber the good, a person has bad karma.

Hindus believe in reincarnation. This is the view that at death the soul always passes into another body. This rebirth is determined by a person's karma. A person with bad karma will be reborn as a lower person or even as an animal or insect. (For this reason, most Hindus are strict vegetarians.) This is not viewed as a punishment, just cause and effect. A person with good karma will return to an improved position in life. Salvation occurs when one is finally released from this continuous wheel of rebirth. A Hindu is "saved" when the cycle is broken because the person is cleansed of earthly sins and the spirit is united with Brahman.

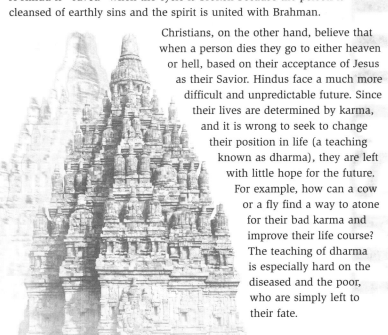

Christians, on the other hand, believe that when a person dies they go to either heaven or hell, based on their acceptance of Jesus as their Savior. Hindus face a much more difficult and unpredictable future. Since their lives are determined by karma, and it is wrong to seek to change their position in life (a teaching known as dharma), they are left with little hope for the future. For example, how can a cow or a fly find a way to atone for their bad karma and improve their life course? The teaching of dharma is especially hard on the diseased and the poor, who are simply left to their fate.

A Life of Duty

Hindus, in an attempt to develop good karma, live a punishing life of duty. Salvation, called *moksha,* can take many lifetimes and is gained through philosophy or knowledge, works of religious observance such as meditation and yoga, and devotion through image worship. Followers, called *yogi,* inflict pain on themselves in search of a mystical experience that will somehow further their understanding.

Some disciples of Hinduism wear orange robes and have shaved heads. They practice yoga—doing chants, postures, and breathing exercises while meditating on a phrase or picture.

Idols

Most Hindu households contain a shrine with idols. As an act of devotion, the worshipper anoints the god while reciting texts, then sits to meditate. Incense is lit and flowers and food are then placed before the shrine.

Duty vs. Unending Love

Unlike the duty-based, frustrating trap Hindus find themselves in, Christianity offers an intimate, loving relationship with a personal God. Christians find grace and salvation through God's goodness, not their own perfect behavior or duty-bound devotion. Hindus offer sacrifices to god in an effort to somehow gain approval. In contrast, Christianity is the only world religion in which God offers a sacrifice to humankind—his own Son, overcoming sin and reconciling people to God through his unending love.

GOD?

God or "Brahman" is a universal spirit that has taken on many different forms. People are part of that spirit and the ultimate goal of Hindus is to be absorbed back into the spirit of Brahman.

JESUS?

Jesus was one of many of god's sons. He was a teacher, or guru. He didn't rise from the dead.

THE WORLD?

The world was created by Brahma. Every living creature is believed to have a soul.

HUMAN BEINGS?

Humans came into existence through Brahman and are thought to be part of god like drops in the sea.

SIN?

There really isn't such a thing as sin, however a person's future depends entirely on his or her present behavior. Bad actions result in future suffering, experienced in the exact same measure (karma).

THE AFTERLIFE?

When a person dies, he or she returns to earth in the form of another living creature determined by karma. The only way to break this cycle of reincarnation is through philosophy or knowledge, works of religious observance, and devotion.

HINDU RELIGIOUS TEXTS INCLUDE:

- The Vedas (written around 1000 B.C.), which contain Hindu law.
- The Great Epics (including the *Bhagavad-Gita*), a collection of great stories.
- The Puranas, which contain mythology from the medieval period.

Suffering, Meditation, AND Right Living

A Closer Look at Buddhism

Who Was Buddha?

An Indian prince named Siddhartha Gautama founded Buddhism. Gautama was born around 560 B.C. and lived a life of luxury in his father's palace. He learned the ways of Hinduism, was married, and had a child. After taking a tour of his father's kingdom, Gautama became very concerned with how people in India were suffering. He left his palace, wife, and child, and set out to understand the problem of suffering.

After meditating under a tree throughout the night, Gautama realized that suffering comes from our own minds and actions. Because of this enlightenment, Siddhartha Gautama became known as the Buddha (the Awakened One). Buddha developed the Four Noble Truths to help guide people through the problem of suffering.

The Four Noble Truths

The Four Noble Truths Gautama developed are

1. People must realize there is suffering in life.

Suffering (*duhkha*) is a natural part of life. There are three types of suffering. The first has to do with natural suffering such as birth, sickness, aging and death. The second type is concerned with how change causes us to suffer. The third type is a result of conditioning or ignorance. As long as we don't understand our state or aren't "enlightened," we will suffer.

2. People must realize the cause for this suffering is their own cravings or desires.

A famous Buddhist called the Dalai Lama says in *The Four Noble Truths,* "If you look carefully, everything beautiful and good, everything that we consider desirable, brings us suffering in the end." Much of Buddhism is concerned with overcoming our desires.

3. Suffering can be overcome or avoided by letting go of the cravings.

The universe is connected. Whenever we act or think, we create a reaction. This process is known as karma. Positive actions create positive karma. Negative actions create negative karma. However, finding enlightenment comes from understanding what it means to empty our minds.

4. We can let go of our cravings by following the Eightfold Path.

We can reach nirvana (bliss), an end to the cycle of birth and rebirth, by following the Eightfold Path. The Eightfold Path consists of right living, right aspirations, right speech, right behavior, right occupation, right effort, right mindfulness, and right meditation.

What's the Difference Between Christianity and Buddhism?

Buddhists don't necessarily believe in any kind of god. Buddhists feel that we can't really know how the universe began and that people who have opinions about our origin can't possibly know the truth. Rather than wasting time on "unanswerable" questions, Buddhists concentrate on dealing with their personal situations.

However, Genesis 1 clearly states that God created the heavens and the earth. While it may be impossible to prove creation, it is certainly important to consider how we came into existence. Ignoring the question altogether could be a very dangerous and detrimental position. The evidence of the existence of a creator is seen all around us. The complexity and beauty of nature, the heart and intelligence of people, and our deepest questions and longings all point to the existence of the Creator.

The primary difference between Buddhism and Christianity is really found in how you look at yourself. If you think you can overcome your desires and sins on your own strength, Buddhism may make some sense. If you believe that it's impossible to make every sin right on your own and to completely overcome your sinful nature on your own, you realize your need for help (see Romans 5:6-15). Thankfully, God offers that very help through his Son, Jesus Christ.

Can They Both Be True?

Many Buddhists (including the Dalai Lama) believe that people should live by whatever faith "system" works for them. While this position feels very comforting to many, it presents some serious problems.

First of all, Jesus claimed that he is *the* way, *the* truth, and *the* life (John 14:6). As C.S. Lewis, the famous writer, once argued, Jesus was either crazy, an evil liar, or telling the truth. If Jesus was crazy, then you really can't buy much of anything he said. It's hard to believe he was lying because he could have avoided being executed simply by changing his story. It doesn't really make sense to say you believe part of what Jesus said, because you'd believe the teachings of a liar or crazy person. Jesus said he was God. Either he was, or there was a serious problem with his thinking.

Secondly, the very cores of Buddhism and Christianity don't line up. A lot of the less-important teachings are compatible. For example, both religions teach that we should avoid hurting others and we should take time to look into our own hearts. But the core of Christianity is that Jesus is God and that he died for our sins. The essence of Christianity says that you can't find forgiveness without Jesus. The heart of Buddhism teaches that we need to look at life and ourselves differently and to change the way we see things to reach nirvana.

The two religions offer two completely different ways of looking at the world. They both have some overlapping truths, but only one of them can be completely true.

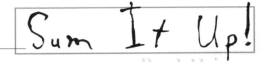
GOD?

There is no god (or if there is, it is unknowable). However, there is a universal force that runs through all things.

JESUS?

Jesus was a man who had good teachings. He may have been an enlightened teacher. He was not god.

THE WORLD?

Zen Buddhists don't give an explanation for the world's existence. They believe that people cannot definitively understand where the universe came from.

HUMAN BEINGS?

Humans have difficulty understanding suffering. By overcoming suffering, humans can reach enlightenment.

SIN?

There really is no such thing as sin. However, people can create bad karma through their thoughts and actions.

THE AFTERLIFE?

Nirvana (bliss) may be reached after complete enlightenment. Many Buddhists believe that one's consciousness will cease to exist after death and that the person will become a part of the energy that makes up the universe.

BUDDHIST RELIGIOUS TEXTS INCLUDE:

• The Tipitaka, the collected writings of Siddhartha Gautama (or the Buddha).

• Buddhists also refer to a variety of writings from enlightened teachers throughout the ages.

Astrology, Enlightenment, AND Mother Earth

A Closer Look at the New Age Movement

The New Age movement is just that—a movement. It is not a religion, in the organized sense of the word. The New Age movement is made up of individuals and organizations that hold to a common set of beliefs and have a passion to see others become "enlightened." Adherents desire to help people get in touch with the "divine" that resides within them.

In the Stars

The New Age movement has roots in Hinduism and in astrology. In fact the term "new age" refers to the coming of a new astrological age (the

"Aquarian age") which will be marked by unity with the cosmos, peace, and a state of utopia on earth. Astrologers believe that humankind exists within evolutionary cycles that last for two hundred years. Each cycle is represented by one of the twelve signs of the zodiac. Each cycle has its own unique characteristics and influences on humankind. Astrologers believe that we are at the end of the age of Pisces, characterized by darkness, violence, and ignorance. We as a human race, they believe, are at the dawning of the Aquarian age, a time of light, love, and enlightenment.

Those who adhere to New Age ideas believe that in order for that age to truly come and change our world, we need to go through a process of enlightenment. Though in Christianity, humanity's essential problem is one of separation from God because of sin, New Age adherents see the problem with humanity today as an issue of ignorance to people's true divine natures. For the New Age follower, everything one sees is made up of the same reality, the same essence (monism)—that essence is god. God is not a personal being, as we see in the Bible, but rather an impersonal force, what some call the "Universal Reality." God is everywhere and everything people see is god (pantheism).

Enlightenment

The goal of the New Age movement, and the key to bringing the Aquarian age into existence is found in what is called enlightenment, self-realization, or god-consciousness. This is the point at which people are fully aware and experience the Ultimate Reality in them. According to Debra Lardie, when people achieve enlightenment, their "sense of personal identity vanishes, they are released from the realm of illusion [and ignorance], and they realize their [inner] divinity."

In the course of enlightenment, New Age followers may experience reincarnation. Whereas the Bible is clear that humans have only one physical lifetime, New Age adherents believe that if they were to die and still not attain full enlightenment, they would come back as another person or creature, seeking to continue the process of perfect enlightenment. Once a person achieves enlightenment, he or she ends the process of reincarnation and is joined to the impersonal cosmic force called god. Those who follow the New Age movement seek out help and guidance on their journey toward enlightenment from those who have died and have finished the journey in a state of full enlightenment. This process of seeking the advice of dead human beings is called channeling, something which God's Word speaks against (see Deuteronomy 18:10-12 and 1 John 4:1-3).

Finding the Personal God

People that are involved in the New Age movement are honestly searching. They are searching for answers because they sense a thirst and hunger in their soul. They are looking for a way to experience God. People that are involved in the New Age movement matter to God. He loves them and desires that they come to know him in a dynamic and personal way. God is not an impersonal force. The God of Scripture is the personal creator of every human heart. He knows us and desires that we know and encounter him.

God does have much to say about the hunger that New Age followers feel. He has much to say about their beliefs. He has even more to say in answer to all their questions. God's Word is truth. It is truth that you can believe in and stake your life upon. God's desire is that we come to know him, the Truth, in a personal and life-altering way—and that we share the truth about Jesus with others, including those in the New Age movement.

What does the New Age Movement teach about...

GOD?

God is an impersonal force, sometimes called a consciousness or an energy. God is *all* and *all* is god. God is the life within all things.

JESUS?

Jesus was an enlightened teacher and is on the same level with other holy men such as the Buddha (Buddhism) and Krishna (Hinduism). New Age adherents see the Christ as a cosmic, divine entity that dwelt for a time in Jesus' body.

THE WORLD?

The earth is a cosmic goddess, sometimes referred to as Mother Earth. Since all is one and god is all, the world and humankind are one and are both divine.

HUMAN BEINGS?

Humankind is god. Because humans are god, they have unlimited potential. Humans, as gods, can create their own realities.

SIN?

Human beings do not have a sin problem; they have a problem of ignorance. Humans are ignorant of their divinity.

THE AFTERLIFE?

Through reincarnation, a person is eventually made perfect and ultimately reunited with the divine god-force. Dead people who are in a state of perfected enlightenment can be contacted via channeling for information and insight.

NEW AGE RELIGIOUS TEXTS INCLUDE:

- Many different sources, such as the Bible and Levi Dowling's *The Aquarian Gospel of Jesus the Christ*.

- The New Age movement also adheres to new revelations revealed through channeling.

Sum It Up!

Judaism

GOD?

God is one and is eternal. He cannot be divided into parts or beings in any way. God is the creator and has revealed himself and his will for people through the law, the prophets, the rabbis' teachings.

JESUS?

Jesus was a good teacher who taught things that were similar to the teachings of other rabbis of his day. He was not divine.

THE WORLD?

The world was created by God.

HUMAN BEINGS?

All human beings were created by God, but the Jews were chosen to be God's special people through whom he would bless the world.

SIN?

People are not born sinful; they have both good and bad inclinations. They have the freedom to choose between right and wrong.

THE AFTERLIFE?

People who generally follow God's teachings and refrain from too much sinning have hope of the resurrection. However, Jewish teachings on the nature of the afterlife are diverse and somewhat vague.

JEWISH RELIGIOUS TEXTS INCLUDE:

- The Torah (or Pentateuch) and the other books of the Old Testament.
- The teachings of the rabbis (the Talmud).

Duty, Obedience, AND Discipline

A Closer Look at Islam

What's the fastest growing religion in the world today?

If you guessed Islam, you're correct! Since 1960, the number of Muslims in the world has tripled, mostly due to population growth in Islamic countries around the world. You can't go far without hearing about Islam, through news articles, movies, or even through popular athletes—but how do you know if what you're hearing really represents the facts? Keep on reading to get a balanced perspective about the basic beliefs of Islam.

Allah

Muslims refer to god as "Allah" and believe that there is no other god besides Allah. They believe that Muhammad was Allah's prophet.

Who Was Muhammad?

Muhammad, the central prophet of the Muslim faith, was born in 570 in Mecca (present-day Saudi Arabia). He was very poor and was orphaned at age six. As he grew older, Muhammad often withdrew from the crowds and the idol worship common in Mecca to a small cave where he could meditate. Muhammad claimed that when he was forty years old, he was in the cave and Allah called his name and spoke to him. Muhammad is believed to have continued receiving revelations from Allah throughout the rest of his life. He wrote down these revelations in a text that is known as the Koran.

At first Muhammad's revelations did not receive a warm reception in Mecca. Many people wondered if the Koran was really from god, so Muhammad challenged them to write a line of Arabic of equal quality and no one could meet his challenge. Nonetheless, Muhammad and his few followers were driven from Mecca and went to live in a nearby city, Medina. (This event, the *Hijrah*, marks the beginning of the Islamic calendar.) In Medina the people accepted Muhammad and Islam, and after several years Muhammad returned to Mecca, conquered the city, and became its leader. Most of the Meccans became Muslims, and over the next several years, Islam spread until the kingdom was larger than the Roman Empire.

The Koran

The Koran is the most sacred Islamic book, though Muslims also highly regard the *Hadith*, a collection of stories and sayings about Muhammad. Though the *Hadith* is an important book, it is not considered to be divinely inspired.

The Koran is not only a central part of religious life, but it is also used to create laws in many Islamic countries. The Koran includes guidelines about how Muslims should live, as well as poetry and information about art and science.

A Different Jesus

On the surface, there are some similarities between the Koran and the Bible. Both include guidelines about how to live and both contain stories about Jesus. But if you look a little deeper, you'll see that these surface similarities are deceiving—though the name "Jesus" is the same, the person being described is very different.

Muslims *do* believe that Jesus was born of the Virgin Mary; in fact, in Islam, Jesus is often referred to as Mary's Son. They believe that he performed many great miracles, such as giving sight to the blind and healing the sick. However, Muslims believe that Jesus did not actually die when he was crucified. Instead, they believe that it only *appeared* as if he had died, when in fact Allah had really taken Jesus' spirit up to heaven before he was killed.

The critical difference, though, is this: Islam teaches that Jesus was one of the greatest prophets that ever lived—but he was not God. The Koran clarifies that not only was Jesus not God, but that the idea of the Trinity is also false. Koran 4:171 says, "The Messiah, the Son of Mary, was only a messenger of Allah...So believe in Allah and His messengers, and say not, "Three"—Cease—[it is] better for you! Allah is only One God."

The Five Pillars

Muslim religious life centers around five obligations for worship, also known as the five pillars of Islam. The first pillar is the *Shahada* or confession of faith: "There is no god but Allah and Muhammad is his prophet." The second pillar is prayer; Muslims must pray in submission to Allah five times a day: before sunrise, between midday and afternoon, in the afternoon, immediately after sunset, and between the time twilight is over and just before dawn. The other pillars of worship include giving money, fasting from sunrise to sunset during Ramadan, and taking a pilgrimage to Mecca. Observing these pillars perfectly and with the right attitude is the key to an afterlife in heaven with Allah.

Heaven or Hell?

Unlike Christianity, Muslims believe that Jesus' death does not play a role in the forgiveness of sins. One of Allah's ninety-nine names in the Koran is "Merciful" and Muslims rely on this mercy, believing that humans are basically good and that Allah will forgive sins when Muslims ask him to. However, to get into heaven, Muslims believe that a person has to do a lot more than simply ask for forgiveness for sins. To reach heaven, a person must resist Satan and perform all of the essential obligations of worship (the five pillars) in an attitude of total surrender to Allah. Those who don't meet these requirements go to hell, a place of eternal torture.

Perfection vs. Grace

The word *Islam* actually means "submission" in Arabic and this requirement of complete submission and perfection in performing the obligations of worship is the key difference between Islam and Christianity.

Is it possible to be perfect? To never miss one of the five daily prayers? To have a completely submissive attitude to Allah at all times?

Humans make mistakes—*no one* is perfect. Muslims who have ever "messed up" on one of these points are facing a big problem—how can they know if they'll go to heaven?

Christians have a hope that is much different than striving to achieve perfection in order to please God. Unlike the focus on dutiful works in Islam, Christianity is based on God's grace. The Bible says in Ephesians 2:8-9, "It is by grace you have been saved, through faith—and this not from yourselves, it is the gift of God—not by works, so that no one can boast." The central hope of Christianity is not what one can *do* to get into heaven—it's what Jesus *did* on the cross. In complete love, Jesus paid the price for sin and offers grace and forgiveness to those who believe in him.

What does
Islam
teach
about...

Sum It Up!
Islam

GOD? There is only one god, Allah, who has no equals. Nothing compares with Allah, as Muslims state in their cry, "Allah is greater."

JESUS? Jesus was a very highly esteemed messenger of Allah. Jesus was one of the greatest prophets but was not God. Jesus did not die but "was made to appear so to them" (Koran 4:157). Allah saved Jesus from the cross by raising him to himself before death.

THE WORLD? The world was created by Allah in six days.

HUMAN BEINGS? Humans were created by Allah to be basically good. They have a special responsibility to care for Allah's creation and are destined for heaven unless they disobey Allah.

SIN? Allah has given humans the choice to obey or disobey his laws. Disobedience is sin.

THE AFTERLIFE? Muslims who perform all the essential obligations in worship with the proper attitude of total submission to Allah will go to paradise (heaven). All others go to hell, a place of everlasting torment.

ISLAMIC RELIGIOUS TEXTS INCLUDE:
- The Koran, which is believed to be the final word of Allah given to humans. Muslims believe that the angel Gabriel gave it directly to Muhammad and it alone is divinely inspired.

- The *Hadith*, collected sayings and acts of the prophet Muhammad, is an important text, but is not considered divinely inspired.

Devoted Followers, UNUSUAL BELIEFS, AND Altered Truths

A Closer Look at Cults

What Exactly Is a Cult?

A cult is a religious group that claims to be Christian but significantly changes or alters at least one of the basic beliefs about who God is, Jesus, the Bible, the nature of humanity, or the nature of sin. There are plenty of religions out there that don't claim or even pretend to be Christian—those are not cults. There are also a variety of Christian denominations and styles of worship, but as long as they agree on basic orthodox beliefs, they're not cults either.

There are a lot of cults in the world today—some are so small that you may never have heard of them, while others are large and growing in popularity. Here you'll have a chance to take a closer look at the beliefs of four well-known groups: Mormons, Jehovah's Witnesses, Christian Scientists, and Unitarian Universalists.

What Mormons Believe

Mormons believe that god was once a man and lived on "an earth" as we do. Because of his right living, he was exalted to his current position as ruler of planet earth. All inhabitants of earth are spirit children of god, as is Jesus. Mormons believe that Jesus came to earth and lived a sinless life to show us the way to eternal exaltation. Jesus' sacrifice on the cross was sufficient to guarantee us resurrection from the dead, but eternal exaltation depends on living a righteous life and keeping a multitude of rules.

Mormons believe that all humans have a pre-mortal existence as spirit creatures with god before coming to earth. And they believe that in the afterlife, if they have followed all the Mormon laws, Mormon men will be eternally exalted, becoming gods themselves and ruling their own "earths." Mormon women have no hope of such exaltation unless they are sealed in marriage to a Mormon man.

Mormon holy writings include the Bible, the *Book of Mormon*, *Doctrine and Covenants*, and *The Pearl of Great Price*. The *Book of Mormon* chronicles the history of early American inhabitants, descendants of the lost tribes of Israel, and Jesus' supposed appearance to them. Interestingly, much of the information about early American inhabitants in the *Book of Mormon* contradicts what most archeologists and anthropologists believe about ancient American civilizations.

What Jehovah's Witnesses Believe

Jehovah's Witnesses do not believe in the Trinity. They believe that the Father is god alone. Jesus, they say, is god's first and supreme creation, and is in fact one and the same as Michael the archangel. Everything else was created by god through Jesus (aka Michael the archangel), god's "junior partner." Jesus' perfect human life and death on earth gives humans the right to perfect life on a paradise earth, but we must earn that prize.

Jehovah's Witnesses believe that only 144,000 anointed followers have achieved eternal salvation, born again as spiritual sons of god to rule with Christ. The rest of true Jehovah's Witnesses believers look forward to eternal life on a paradise earth. However, they have no assurance of that eternal life; it is dependent on keeping many rules. They believe in the Bible, but only in their own New World Translation, which mistranslates, alters, and rewrites verses to make them agree with their own beliefs.

Jehovah's Witnesses believe that a person's soul is contained in his blood; for this reason they are against blood transfusions because that would create a mixing of people's souls. They do not celebrate birthdays, Christmas, or other holidays because they consider such celebrations pagan in nature and idolatrous.

What Christian Scientists Believe

Christian Scientists follow the teachings of Mary Baker Eddy in her book *Science and Health With Key to the Scriptures*. This book teaches that humans and God are one in being, a single spiritual entity. Sickness, sin, and death are not real—they are only illusions. Only spiritual things are real. God exists only as a nebulous concept of "good." Jesus does not provide salvation, but only an example of love and how to live.

Christian Scientists concentrate on healing, which involves a mind over matter trick of convincing oneself that a sickness or evil does not exist. They don't believe in heaven or hell, except as states of mind experienced here and now, as well as after death.

What Unitarian Universalists Believe

Unitarian Universalists do not claim to necessarily have any beliefs in common. They believe in reason and experience and encourage everyone to believe whatever they want. Some believe in god, some don't, and some believe in gods from other religions. They believe more in the fruits of religion than in its doctrine. Christian traits such as service, justice, hope, tolerance, personal growth, increased wisdom, peace, and compassion are important goals for Unitarian Universalists.

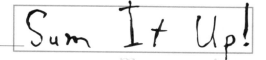

Sum It Up!

Mormonism

GOD?

God was once a man and lived on "an earth." God is one of many gods.

JESUS?

Jesus lived as a sinless human to show people the way to earn their own exaltation.

THE WORLD?

The world was created by god so he could give his spirit children human life and the chance of eternal exaltation.

HUMAN BEINGS?

People are god's spirit children, placed on earth in human form to attain eternal exaltation.

SIN?

Adam's sin actually fulfilled God's purpose of populating the earth. Humans must follow many laws to earn exaltation.

THE AFTERLIFE?

Faithful Mormon men will be exalted and become gods, ruling and populating their own earths. Women can be exalted only if sealed in marriage to a Mormon man.

MORMON RELIGIOUS TEXTS INCLUDE:

- The Bible.
- *Book of Mormon.*
- *Doctrine and Covenants.*
- *The Pearl of Great Price.*

What do
Jehovah's
Witnesses
teach
about...

Sum It Up!

Jehovah's Witnesses

GOD?

God the Father is god alone. Jesus is god's first creation and is the same as Michael the archangel. The Holy Spirit is god's impersonal, active energy force.

JESUS?

Jesus is god's created son. Jesus was a perfect human being, but was not God. His death and resurrection earned humans the right to perfect life on earth.

THE WORLD?

The world was created by god as a paradise for perfect human existence.

HUMAN BEINGS?

Humans were created by god to live a perfect life on a paradise earth.

SIN?

All human beings are sinful because of Adam's sin. Jesus' perfect human life and death gives humans the right to perfect life on a paradise earth, but people must earn that prize by living rightly.

THE AFTERLIFE?

Only 144,000 anointed people will enjoy rebirth as god's spiritual children and rule with him in heaven. Other faithful Jehovah's Witnesses followers that obey all the laws have a chance to live forever on a paradise earth. All others are destroyed.

JEHOVIAH'S WITNESSES RELIGIOUS TEXTS INCLUDE:

- The New World Translation of the Bible.
- Publications from the Watchtower Bible and Tract Society.

So What's THE Truth?

A Closer Look at Christianity

$2 + 2 = 4$

It does not equal five. It does not equal three. Two plus two equals four.

There are countless spiritual options out there—many more than those covered in this booklet—and they all offer a version of "the truth." On the surface they may look similar. After all, most religions teach that people should be good, right? That we should try not to hurt others and that we should make good choices?

Well, *yeah*. But there's much more to those religious beliefs than just what you see on the surface. As you've read, the major religions in the world are *not* the same. There are fundamental differences that make them unique—teachings that set them apart from each other. What they believe about God, the world, Jesus, human beings, and how sin affects our relationship with God is important to consider. And their differences on these issues are big ones.

Imagine a person who claims that two plus two equals seven and another person who claims that it equals four. Would you think that both of them were right? Obviously not. Deep in our hearts we know that there is only one truth…and we were created to search for it and to know it.

Jesus once said, "I am the way and the truth and the life" (John 14:6a). His words and the teachings about him in the Bible lead us to the ultimate truth—the truth that we can have a personal relationship with a holy God who loves us deeply. The truth that Jesus died for us on the cross and rose from the dead to pay the penalty for our sins. The truth that faith in Jesus allows us to find forgiveness and freedom from sin and guilt. The truth that we can live abundant lives and experience intimacy with God.

Listen to these words of Jesus: "If you hold to my teaching, you are really my disciples. Then you will know the truth, and the truth will set you free" (John 8:31-32).

If you have questions about Christianity, talk with your pastor or a trusted Christian friend.

What does Christianity teach about...	Sum It Up!

GOD?

God is the ruler of all and exists as one God in three persons: the Father, the Son, and the Holy Spirit. God is the eternal creator of the universe in which we live. God reveals himself to human beings through the Bible and through creation.

JESUS?

Jesus was 100 percent God and 100 percent man. He is God's Son and part of the Trinity. Jesus died on a cross and was resurrected for the forgiveness of sins.

THE WORLD?

The world was created by God.

HUMAN BEINGS?

Humans were created by God for relationship with him. Each person is separated from God by sin but can find forgiveness and a restored relationship with God through faith in Jesus.

SIN?

All human beings are sinful and that sin separates them from God.

THE AFTERLIFE?

Human beings who have a faith relationship with Jesus will go to heaven when they die and spend eternity with God. Those who do not place their faith in Jesus will be separated from God in hell.

CHRISTIAN RELIGIOUS TEXT:

• The Bible.